Little Red Dragon

Written by Tony Mitton

Illustrated by Dom Mansell

Rigby

Little Red Dragon
puffs up her chest.

She picks up twigs
and she makes a little nest.

"Yes!" says the dragon.
"It's a neat little nest.
Now it's time to give it
the hip-hop test."

First she hops out.

Then she hops in.

Then she makes it tidy
as a neat new pin.

She flies to the east.

She flies to the west.

Then she comes back
to take a little rest.

Little Red Dragon
hops from her nest.
She sits on a rock
with a little green guest.

A man near the nest
has a great big net.
He wants to catch the dragon
to keep as a pet.

The dragon flaps her wings.

She ruffles her crest.

She puffs out smoke, saying, "Nets are a pest!"

She cocks her head.
She puffs up her chest.
"I'll give that man
a catching test."

She hops from the rock
to land on a log.
She grins at a fish.
She winks at the frog.

The man makes a jump.
The dragon goes **hop!**

The dragon flies up,
but the man goes *plop!*

Little Red Dragon,
back in her nest,
sits there boasting,
"Dragons are best!"